THE BRITISH

The British

The National Character Observed

by PONT

DUCKWORTH

This edition published in 2024 by Duckworth,
an imprint of Duckworth Books Ltd,
1 Golden Court, Richmond, TW9 1EU, United Kingdom
www.duckworthbooks.co.uk

First published in 2011 by Duckworth Overlook

All rights reserved. No part of this publication
may be reproduced, stored in a retrieval system, or
transmitted, in any form or by any means, electronic,
mechanical, photocopying, recording or otherwise,
without the prior permission of the publisher.

The right of Duckworth to be identified as the copyright holder of
this edition has been asserted in accordance with
the Copyright, Design and Patents Act 1998.

A catalogue record for this book is available
from the British Library

ISBN 978-0-7156-5507-8

Printed and bound in the UK
by Bell and Bain Ltd, Glasgow

Contents

The British Character / 1

At Home / 77

Popular Misconceptions / 89

Miscellaneous Cartoons / 103

Index of Illustrations / 163

The British Character

Adaptability to foreign conditions

4th April 1934

Reserve

25th April 1934

The 'Sea Sense'

16th May 1934

Failure to appreciate good music

29th August 1934

Love of open-air sports

19th September 1934

Love of dumb animals

10th October 1934

Skill at foreign languages

17th October 1934

Love of games

7th December 1934

Absence of the gift for cooking

12th December 1934

Absence of the gift of conversation

18th September 1935

Love of writing letters to *The Times*

23rd October 1935

The importance of tea

30th October 1935

Indispensability of golf

13th November 1935

The exaltation of cleanliness

18th March 1936

Passion for the antique

25th March 1936

Enthusiasm for hunting

8th April 1936

Importance of not being an alien

15th April 1936

Determination not to preserve the rural amenities

22nd April 1936

Enthusiasm for gardening

29th April 1936

The attitude towards fresh air

6th May 1936

Attitude towards hostesses

27th May 1936

Importance of exercise

10th June 1936

The gift for water colours

1st July 1936

Keen interest in historic houses

8th July 1936

Keen interest in the weather

29th July 1936

Love of detective fiction

19th August 1936

Inability of British broadcasting announcers to speak English

30th September 1936

Political apathy

14th October 1936

Absolute indispensability of bacon and eggs for breakfast

11th November 1936

Love of arriving late at theatrical productions

18th November 1936

Refusal to admit defeat

25th November 1936

Extraordinary propensity of the farmers to grumble

9th December 1936

Strong tendency to become doggy

16th December 1936

Untitled

30th December 1936

Importance of not being intellectual

6th January 1937

Love of never throwing anything away

20th January 1937

Fondness for laughing at our own anecdotes

10th February 1937

Aptitude for building Empire

17th February 1937

Fondness for travel

3rd March 1937

Absence of ideas for meals

24th March 1937

Partiality for open fires

31st March 1937

The importance of breeding

7th April 1937

Tendency to be embarrassed by foreign currencies

14th April 1937

Curiosity

21st April 1937

Love of keeping calm

5th May 1937

A reverential attitude towards bridge?

26th May 1937

Proneness to superstition

2nd June 1937

A weakness for oak beams

9th June 1937

Fondness for cricket

16th June 1937

A tendency to put things away safely

23rd June 1937

Importance of being athletic

30th June 1937

Preference for driving on the crown of the road

7th July 1937

Absence of enthusiasm for answering letters

14th July 1937

Patience

28th July 1937

Love of travelling alone

4th August 1937

A tendency to be hearty

18th August 1937

Imperialism

25th August 1937

Love of everything French

1st September 1937

A tendency to learn the piano when young

29th September 1937

A tendency to think things not so good as they used to be

6th October 1937

Tendency not to know what to do on Sundays

20th October 1937

Love of being horsey

10th November 1937

Ability to manage for oneself on Sunday evening

17th November 1937

A weakness for mid-morning nourishment

24th November 1937

Patience in adversity

1st December 1937

A disinclination to sparkle

8th December 1937

A tendency to put off till the last minute

5th January 1938

Ability to be ruthless

19th January 1938

A tendency to leave the washing up till later

26th January 1938

A disinclination ever to go anywhere

2nd February 1938

A keen curiosity about the future

9th February 1938

The importance of news

16th February 1938

Attitude towards insomnia

23rd February 1938

At Home

The happy farmer

20th July 1938

The successful doctor

27th July 1938

The fag

24th August 1938

Country folk

21st September 1938

The singer

26th October 1938

The epicure

14th December 1938

The neurotic

4th January 1939

The bachelor

1st February 1939

The house-proud wife

12th April 1939

Popular Misconceptions

British business methods

23rd November 1938

Life among the really rich

8th February 1939

Life in the flat above

15th February 1939

Life in the democracies

24th May 1939

The people behind

21st June 1939

The English Channel

5th July 1939

How to win the war

29th November 1939

Life in the B.E.F.

13th December 1939

(In Germany) The Germans

14th February 1940

How to fill the troops with keenness

Unpublished

A wagon-lit train at speed

Unpublished

Miscellaneous Cartoons

"My dear, how I pity you, all cooped up in London. As I sit writing this there is nothing to be seen anywhere but miles of open sea."

31st August 1932

"Another restless night, Stevens."

7th August 1935

News

28th August 1935

"Did I really understand you, Miss Wilson, to use the expression, 'a cosy nook', in connection with the house you wish me to design for you?"

5th February 1936

"Anyway, the young man last year never forgot to tell us when to put our waterproofs on."

2nd September 1936

"Of course, we must face facts. It's going to mean waiting."

12th May 1937

"There will be nineteen extra to lunch today."

23rd June 1937

"I wonder if there is a really nice little boy in the room who would like to run upstairs and look for Mummy's spectacles."

21st July 1937

Don't be silly, darling, would mother be likely to say it did if it didn't?"

18th August 1937

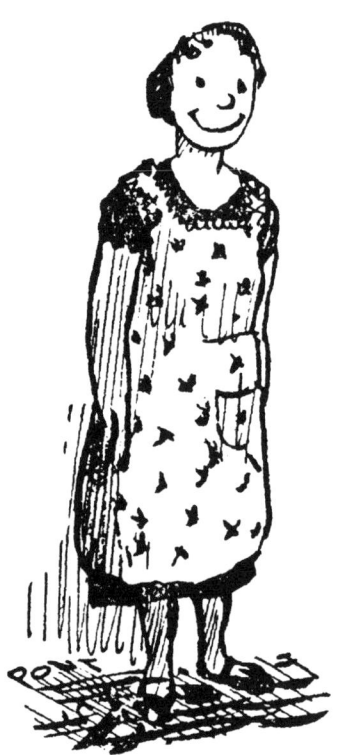

"I expect that was today's I was lighting the fire with."

25th August 1937

"… and the doctors *all* said they'd *never* seen one like it."

25th August 1937

"Once more unto the breach, dear friends, once more …"

1st September 1937

"Precisely the same as they said about poor Frederic, my dear,
and he scarcely lasted a week"

8th September 1937

"Don't trouble, George, dear, I can manage quite well without it."

22nd September 1937

"To be perfectly frank, my dear lady, no I can't hear a 'funny humming noise.'"

13th October 1937

"It's quite all right, dear, I can manage perfectly well without them – honestly I can."

20th October 1937

"The fact is, my dear fellow – and you may as well admit it –
we're not so young as we were forty years ago."

27th October 1937

This is Mr. Clothesbrush –   *and Miss Thomson –*   *and Professor Churcher, who invented the Churchur –*   *and Captain Elephantsare-bigtoday –*

and Miss Vincent –   *and Miss Carter –*   *and Lady Heigh-Ho –*   *and my brother –*

Cocktails 6 till 8

1st November 1937

and Sir William Globbglob, the famous Gloshsush –   *and my other brother –*   *and Miss Thomson –*   *and Miss Turnedoutatslough (I expect you saw her in "Seven nines are eighty-four") –*

and the Dean of Whynot-arresther –   *and of course my Mother –*   *and Mr. Passdownthecar-please, whom you met last time –*   *and now I'm sure you would like something to drink*

Cocktails 6 till 8

1st November 1937

"He says it's not for sale, My Lord."

3rd November 1937

"Sometimes I think they understand every word we say."

10th November 1937

"There are times when I really begin to wonder if all this is worth while."

1st December 1937

"... and then pour the boiling water out of the kettle into the teapot."

19th January 1938

"It seems ridiculous that by this time nobody has thought of an easier way to do these."

19th January 1938

"You can't marry Greta Garbo until you grow up,
so do stop being a baby about it."

26th January 1938

"I've just been wondering, dear, if I don't prefer the piano in the up-stairs room after all."

2nd February 1938

"It's *youth* you need in a business like yours, Mr Zinkbaum.
Youth, with its imagination, drive and enthusiasm."

16th February 1938

"Would you rather I didn't mention the fatal accident?"

23rd March 1938

"Well, and what can you talk about?"

30th March 1938

"And, now, will you open it or shall I?"

6th April 1938

"Tell me – are you a believer in elemental disproportion or de-energised statistics, or do you just stick to the Propkoffer theory?"

13th April 1938

"... 'This looks to me like "Dead-face" Anderson's work,' gasped Detective-Inspector Watkins, eyeing the corpse in the bath ..."

27th April 1938

Domestic difference

11th May 1938

Untitled

30th May 1938

Untitled

30th May 1938

"What I say is that wild flowers don't belong to anybody – see?"

15th June 1938

"There's a most unusual-looking bird on the lawn."

16th November 1938

"Mr Sparks, dear … *longing* to meet you."

7th December 1938

"And now in return we want you to *promise* to bring all your family to stay with us on Saturday week."

31st December 1938

Half-an-hour's rest after meals

11th January 1939

"If you take my advice you won't go upstairs to her. There's nothing wrong; she's only crying because she just wants someone to go and talk to her."

18th January 1939

Tendency among business-men to believe in doing business over lunch

1st March 1939

The gentlemen were all at school together

15th March 1939

"Please, something which won't make me think."

19th April 1939

"I wonder what sort of people find time to look at this sort of rubbish."

3rd May 1939

"Ladies and gentlemen,   these   are troubled times …   We see to-day   this great Empire   upon which

the sun   for so long   etc . . . .   On every side   there are grave   and

Untitled

14th June 1939

horrible *dangers …* *Civilisation is tottering …* *and when* *one looks to the future* *etc . . . .*

I have much pleasure in proposing the toast of –   *the Happy Pair."*

Untitled

14th June 1939

"My parents have a theory about bringing up children."

23rd August 1939

"He says he done it all to save his *face*. Well, well."

27th September 1939

"This is Mummy –   and Daddy –   and Granny –

and Aunti B. –   and Uncle Tom. –   and my brother Alec –

and my sister Winifred and her husband Jack –   and little Stuart –   and dear old Emily –

Meeting the family

6th November 1939

and Mary, my little sister –

and darling *Mrs. Perks –*

and Cousin Clara –

and my eldest brother, Robert –

and Mr. Bossy-Wing–

and Great-Grandfather Foster–

and Towzer –

and Dickey …

Now, darling, whatever is *the matter?"*

Meeting the family

6th November 1939

"Now tell us, Frank dear, what are the next moves in the war?"

3rd April 1940

"It never fails to amaze me how these taxi-drivers find their way about at night."

17th July 1940

"… and not only decorative, they're loaded."

4th September 1940

"I'm perfectly aware of that."

11th September 1940

I first heard old Mrs Todd at the post office telling somebody –

then Mr Brewis told me himself;

Miss Greer came out with the same story –

and I thought little Miss Hopstead was going to take a fit when she told me.

Doctor Gregory had a completely different version of the same thing –

and as for Admiral Stoker…

Col. Chargem and his friend could talk of nothing else –

Young Whatshisname was full of it –

The Saturday morning rumour

4th November 1940

| so were the people in the bank. | The Vicar was booming about it all over the place – | and Mrs. Trent had, as usual, got the whole thing mixed up. | Vera Prestwood said her father had gone to bed immediately when he heard it |

But old Clogwheels said he had expected worse.

Frank ran right across the road to tell me –

and even the people at the Wilsons' wanted to know what I thought.

But I am not going to tell YOU what it was, because I *never* repeat rumours.

The Saturday morning rumour

4th November 1940

"I suppose you know you're doing that all wrong."

4th December 1940

Index of Illustrations

The British Character

A disinclination ever to go anywhere	2nd February 1938	72
A disinclination to sparkle	8th December 1937	68
A keen curiosity about the future	9th February 1938	73
A reverential attitude towards bridge?	26th May 1937	48
A tendency to be hearty	18th August 1937	58
A tendency to learn the piano when young	29th September 1937	61
A tendency to leave the washing up till later	26th January 1938	71
A tendency to put off till the last minute	5th January 1938	69
A tendency to put things away safely	23rd June 1937	52
A tendency to think things not so good as they used to be	6th October 1937	62
A weakness for mid-morning nourishment	24th November 1937	66
A weakness for oak beams	9th June 1937	50
Ability to be ruthless	19th January 1938	70
Ability to manage for oneself on Sunday evening	17th November 1937	65
Absence of enthusiasm for answering letters	14th July 1937	55
Absence of ideas for meals	24th March 1937	42
Absence of the gift for cooking	12th December 1934	11
Absence of the gift of conversation	18th September 1935	12
Absolute indispensability of bacon and eggs for breakfast	11th November 1936	31
Adaptability to foreign conditions	4th April 1934	3
Aptitude for building Empire	17th February 1937	40
Attitude towards hostesses	27th May 1936	23
Attitude towards insomnia	23rd February 1938	75
Curiosity	21st April 1937	46
Determination not to preserve the rural amenities	22nd April 1936	20
Enthusiasm for gardening	29th April 1936	21
Enthusiasm for hunting	8th April 1936	18
Extraordinary propensity of the farmers to grumble	9th December 1936	34
Failure to appreciate good music	29th August 1934	6

Fondness for cricket	16th June 1937	51
Fondness for laughing at our own anecdotes	10th February 1937	39
Fondness for travel	3rd March 1937	41
Imperialism	25th August 1937	59
Importance of being athletic	30th June 1937	53
Importance of exercise	10th June 1936	24
Importance of not being an alien	15th April 1936	19
Importance of not being intellectual	6th January 1937	37
Inability of British broadcasting announcers to speak English	30th September 1936	29
Indispensability of golf	13th November 1935	15
Keen interest in historic houses	8th July 1936	26
Keen interest in the weather	29th July 1936	27
Love of arriving late at theatrical productions	18th November 1936	32
Love of being horsey	10th November 1937	64
Love of detective fiction	19th August 1936	28
Love of dumb animals	10th October 1934	8
Love of everything French	1st September 1937	60
Love of games	7th December 1934	10
Love of keeping calm	5th May 1937	47
Love of never throwing anything away	20th January 1937	38
Love of open-air sports	19th September 1934	7
Love of travelling alone	4th August 1937	57
Love of writing letters to *The Times*	23rd October 1935	13
Partiality for open fires	31st March 1937	43
Passion for the antique	25th March 1936	17
Patience	28th July 1937	56
Patience in adversity	1st December 1937	67
Political apathy	14th October 1936	30
Preference for driving on the crown of the road	7th July 1937	54
Proneness to superstition	2nd June 1937	49
Refusal to admit defeat	25th November 1936	33
Reserve	25th April 1934	4
Skill at foreign languages	17th October 1934	9
Strong tendency to become doggy	16th December 1936	35
Tendency not to know what to do on Sundays	20th October 1937	63
Tendency to be embarrassed by foreign currencies	14th April 1937	45

The attitude towards fresh air	6th May 1936	22
The exaltation of cleanliness	18th March 1936	16
The gift for water colours	1st July 1936	25
The importance of breeding	7th April 1937	44
The importance of news	16th February 1938	74
The importance of tea	30th October 1935	14
The 'Sea Sense'	16th May 1934	5
Untitled	30th December 1936	36

At Home

Country folk	21st September 1938	82
The bachelor	1st February 1939	86
The epicure	14th December 1938	84
The fag	24th August 1938	81
The happy farmer	20th July 1938	79
The house-proud wife	12th April 1939	87
The neurotic	4th January 1939	85
The singer	26th October 1938	83
The successful doctor	27th July 1938	80

Popular Misconceptions

(In Germany) The Germans	14th February 1940	99
A wagon-lit train at speed	Unpublished	101
British business methods	23rd November 1938	91
How to fill the troops with keenness	Unpublished	100
How to win the war	29th November 1939	97
Life among the really rich	8th February 1939	92
Life in the B.E.F.	13th December 1939	98
Life in the democracies	24th May 1939	94
Life in the flat above	15th February 1939	93
The English Channel	5th July 1939	96
The people behind	21st June 1939	95

Miscellaneous Cartoons

"… and not only decorative, they're loaded."	4th September 1940	158
"… and the doctors *all* said they'd *never* seen one like it."	25th August 1937	115
"… and then pour the boiling water out of the kettle into the teapot."	19th January 1938	127
"… 'This looks to me like "Dead-face" Anderson's work,' gasped Detective-Inspector Watkins, eyeing the corpse in the bath …"	27th April 1938	136
"And now in return we want you to *promise* to bring all your family to stay with us on Saturday week."	31st December 1938	143
"And, now, will you open it or shall I?"	6th April 1938	134
"Another restless night, Stevens."	7th August 1935	106
"Anyway, the young man last year never forgot to tell us when to put our waterproofs on."	2nd September 1936	109
"Did I really understand you, Miss Wilson, to use the expression, 'a cosy nook', in connection with the house you wish me to design for you?"	5th February 1936	108
"Don't be silly, darling, would mother be likely to say it did if it didn't?"	18th August 1937	113
"Don't trouble, George, dear, I can manage quite well without it."	22nd September 1937	118
"He says he done it all to save his *face*. Well, well."	27th September 1939	153
"He says it's not for sale, My Lord."	3rd November 1937	124
"I expect that was today's I was lighting the fire with."	25th August 1937	114
"I suppose you know you're doing that all wrong."	4th December 1940	162
"I wonder if there is a really nice little boy in the room who would like to run upstairs and look for Mummy's spectacles."	21st July 1937	112
"I wonder what sort of people find time to look at this sort of rubbish."	3rd May 1939	149
"If you take my advice you won't go upstairs to her. There's nothing wrong; she's only crying because she just wants someone to go and talk to her."	18th January 1939	145
"I'm perfectly aware of that."	11th September 1940	159
"It never fails to amaze me how these taxi-drivers find their way about at night."	17th July 1940	157
"It seems ridiculous that by this time nobody has thought of an easier way to do these."	19th January 1938	128

"It's quite all right, dear, I can manage perfectly well without them – honestly I can."	20th October 1937	120
"It's *youth* you need in a business like yours, Mr Zinkbaum. Youth, with its imagination, drive and enthusiasm."	16th February 1938	131
"I've just been wondering, dear, if I don't prefer the piano in the up-stairs room after all."	2nd February 1938	130
"Mr Sparks, dear … *longing* to meet you."	7th December 1938	142
"My dear, how I pity you, all cooped up in London. As I sit writing this there is nothing to be seen anywhere but miles of open sea."	31st August 1932	105
"My parents have a theory about bringing up children."	23rd August 1939	152
"Now tell us, Frank dear, what are the next moves in the war?"	3rd April 1940	156
"Of course, we must face facts. It's going to mean waiting."	12th May 1937	110
"Once more unto the breach, dear friends, once more …"	1st September 1937	116
"Please, something which won't make me think."	19th April 1939	148
"Precisely the same as they said about poor Frederic, my dear, and he scarcely lasted a week."	8th September 1937	117
"Sometimes I think they understand every word we say."	10th November 1937	125
"Tell me – are you a believer in elemental disproportion or de-energised statics, or do you just stick to the Propkoffer theory?"	13th April 1938	135
"The fact is, my dear fellow – and you may as well admit it – we're not so young as we were forty years ago."	27th October 1937	121
"There are times when I really begin to wonder if all this is worth while."	1st December 1937	126
"There will be nineteen extra to lunch today."	23rd June 1937	111
"There's a most unusual-looking bird on the lawn."	16th November 1938	141
"To be perfectly frank, my dear lady, no I can't hear a 'funny humming noise.'"	13th October 1937	119
"Well, and what can you talk about?"	30th March 1938	133
"What I say is that wild flowers don't belong to anybody – see?"	15th June 1938	140
"Would you rather I didn't mention the fatal accident?"	23rd March 1938	132
"You can't marry Greta Garbo until you grow up, so do stop being a baby about it."	26th January 1938	129
Cocktails 6 till 8	1st November 1937	122–123
Domestic difference	11th May 1938	137
Half-an-hour's rest after meals	11th January 1939	144
Meeting the family	6th November 1939	154–155

News	28th August 1935	107
Tendency among business-men to believe in doing business over lunch	1st March 1939	146
The gentlemen were all at school together	15th March 1939	147
The Saturday morning rumour	4th November 1940	160–161
Untitled	30th May 1938	138–139
Untitled	14th June 1939	150–151